Brad Poetry Collection

Brad Kong

Disclaimer

The **graphics** on this book cover and poetry images are strictly from Edit.org. I use the site's template to design my covers; it provides book cover templates with its copy-righted images to writers who paid "annual memberships."

I do have three proofs of my **membership** to Edit.org, **payment receipt** for the membership through Paypal and **reference** address to the image of the site. I am writing this because I received emails regarding my "book cover images" twice; both cases were resolved within a day. I decided to stick only to my own or edit.org's images since I cannot keep getting copyright emails. If you have any issue regarding my cover art, feel free to contact me: I will be more than happy to provide the three proofs again.

Also by Brad Kong

UnBrokable* series:

UnBrokable* I (Chapter 1 to 10)
UnBrokable* II (Chapter 11 to 20)
UnBrokable* III (Chapter 21 to 30)
UnBrokable* IV (Chapter 31 to 40)
UnBrokable* V (Chapter 41 to 50)

UnBrokable* I Prequel

Preliminary series:

Introduction to UnBrokable*
UnBrokable* I (Chapter 1 to 10)
UnBrokable* II (Chapter 11 to 20)
UnBrokable* III (Chapter 21 to 30)
UnBrokable* IV (Chapter 31 to 40)
UnBrokable* V (Chapter 41 to 50)
UnBrokable* VI (Chapter 51 to 60)
UnBrokable* VII (Chapter 61 to 70)
UnBrokable* VIII (Chapter 71 to 80)
UnBrokable* (Chapter 1 to 80)

Drafts series:

Introduction to UnBrokable* (Chapter 1 to 5)
Intro to UnBrokable* Large Print
UnBrokable* I (Chapter 1 to 10)
UnBrokable* II (Chapter 11 to 20)
UnBrokable* III (Chapter 21 to 30)
UnBrokable* IV (Chapter 31 to 40)

Brad Short Story Collection I:

Brad Short Story Collection II:

Brad Short Story Collection III:

This poetry collection includes 8 books.

Growing with You

with

You

(Poetry Book 1)

On Instagram:

You have beautiful smile,
but your eyes are always sad.
All of them – glowing in moisture.

What happened to you?

What have you been through going up there?

I've heard of rumors, suspects and gossip.
My personal experiences and guesses.

Have you been through it all?

Has it been worth it?

Answering machine:

It has been more than 10 years.
Sad voice in the answering machine.

Maybe life makes us sad.

Not a teenager, but a woman in 30s.
You have been eroded
and tired of giving more favors.

As soon as I heard it,
I could tell you have been through a lot.

Dear woman:

I grow with you.

I am getting old,
but, at the same time, growing with you.

We learn to grow a little everyday.

Thanks to you,
I had a chance to have a family.

Yuna is growing, too.

Rainy:

I like rainy days.

Taking breaths from hectic daily life.
A little break.

A little pause.

Grass smells.
Mild tapping sounds.
Cooler breezes.

I am glad I don't have to go to work.
The biggest blessing in my life.

Little money I have –
enough for a small family living.

No car:

I am glad I don't have a car.
A big relief not to have that ownership.

No one in my family will create a car accident.

Not my daughter,
not my wife,
not me.

We are waiting for the Waymo Robo taxi now.

I cannot do everything on my own –
I have a perfect driving record,
but decided to let it go.

Oscar:

Buffalo SPCA in 2003.

The first day I saw you –

you were 3 months old
standing in front of a cage,
wondering what a car key was like.

We had fun.
We helped each other.
My cold lonesome apartment started filling with joy
after you moved in.

My girlfriend, who was far away, loved you to death.
She became my wife and we have a daughter.

Fast forward 17 years.
Blood cancer.

You were gone in 2020,
while all three of us watched.

Five years has been passed,
but I still miss you.

Chuncheon:

Chuncheon –
2 hours from Seoul.
Population 200,000.
A very small city.

I love small cities in Korea.

Everything is cheaper
and everyone is kind.

Most of all,
I felt like it's OK not to be great.

I felt the city accepted me as who I am.

Great universities –
I had the best 4 years of my life there.

I left my heart.
Someday I will get it back.
Hopefully longer.

Embracing My Poverty

(Poetry Book 2)

Embracing My Poverty:

A cold apartment in Buffalo, NY in 2005.
One bedroom.
$430 rent a month.
Amazingly long winters.

Massive snow.

It's hard to be poor these days –
less physically, more mentally.

The feeling of deprivation and shame.
Emptiness.
Even vengeance.

However, when we give up showing off,
our lives get much easier and comfortable,
instantly.

When we choose not to join
the instinctive competition of comparisons,
especially while we have money,
our life soon turns into heaven.

One day, I realized my poverty is not a real one.
I wasn't hungry or cold.
I just didn't drive a Mercedes.

Wearing inexpensive, but neat winter coats.
Riding Uber,
instead of driving Cadillac myself.

I decided to embrace my poverty –
accepting my brokeness.

When I intended to become a "poor one,"
while sitting on my savings,

I felt really comfy –
comfier than ever.

This is happiness –
the true one,
not the fake ones.

Dishwashing:

The nursing home near my place.
Full time dishwasher.
It felt ridiculous to apply for the job in my 40s.

Early in the morning.
Always too much.
A mountainous amount of dishes and pots.
I felt managers and cooks disregarded me.
They pushed me to move fast.
Always small pay.

Roza.
An uneducated, but aggressive Cuban cook.
No wonder why she got divorced three times.
Five kids.

Carlos.
An unnecessarily rude Mexican sous chef.
Stupid to buy a Lexus with his meager wage.
Feeding three children.
Got fired in the end.

Always tired.
Always got interrupted.
I hated to move back to work after having lunch,
which was why I often skipped it.

The nursing home filed bankruptcy,

a year after I quit the job.

Joe:

A nice fat White guy.
Dishwasher.
Two jobs.
4 children to feed.
Working 5:00 AM till 10:00 PM everyday.

He got married at 42,
but I don't know why he rushed to have that many kids.
His situation could have been better with fewer offspring.

Too good,
so apparently he forgave hostile coworkers.
He never complained about unfairness.
So generous that he always stopped his car
to pick me up on the street.

I felt sorry for him.

I hope he wins the lottery.

Septemberfest:

Schaumburg.
A little known gem in Chicagoland.
A neat, sweet small town.
Great libraries.
Shopping malls.
A sculpture park.

A local festival in Autumn.

Concerts.
Night markets.
Circus rides.
Craft tents.
Beers.
All kinds of strange people from everywhere.

Always fun.

It's OK to be a loser:

There is no winner or loser,
to begin with.

However,
there are people taking advantage of competitions.
They push you to work more.
Most of us follow along.

Sometimes,
We make far more money than we need.
Often blindly.

We waste life away.

Snow

on the

Back Alley

(Poetry Book 3)

Snow on the Back Alley:

A cold lonely night.
Quiet.

A small studio.
Vinyl covered windows.
Snow truck sounds.
Only warmth was from you.

Poor, but never miserable.
Being with you is always Christmas.

Dream:

I thought I forgot about you —
completely.

In chilling autumn morning,
still thinking about the dream.

Welcome to sanity:

Early in the morning,
before you turn on your modem,
before turning on your smartphone.

Have some time to think.
Have some time to read.

Stop frying your eyes.
Stop getting headaches.

Gelato:

Italians must be geniuses.
They invented a lot of colorful things.
Even in ice cream.

Nameless author:

A nameless author like me
needs to write and publish frequently, at least.

Otherwise, my name can disappear completely
on the market in no time.

I ordered a book from another nameless writer
only to make her happy.
I wondered and felt sorry that
some of her YouTube videos have 0 clicks.
So far, I see no response from her on various social media.

If she doesn't care, I don't care.
Maybe this is why she is nameless
despite being a native white Canadian.
Spending most of her time on drinking and disregarding fans.

I still want to read her book,
but I may return within 30 years,
unless I want to keep it.

An Empty Store

(Poetry Book 4)

An Empty Store:

1128 Roselle
850 square feet
in a strip mall
$1,200 a month rent (2006 - 2014)
a video game store
I used to be a boss there.

I dreamed to be rich
soon turned out to be a nightmare
robbery at the gun point
a noisy Jazzercise moved into next door
clangor dispute
finally, I decided not to continue my business there
enough after 8 years.

After I am gone
an "European door sales" came in
I wondered why it's there
instead of next to Home depot.

After it's gone,
women's clothing shop came in
I visited there with my daughter once
she said the rent was $2,000 a month, then.

After it's gone,
a "children's clothing" came in
soon turned into a Polish craft shop.

That's also gone
a new "organic dog food"
is about to move in now
a bit empty at this moment.

The space is not far from my home
whenever I see it
I feel nostalgic
I gave my heart and soul there
the most enthusiastic 8 years.

It wasn't entirely my fault
as it seems nothing really survives there
I am sad, but relieved.

I forgive myself a little.

Victory Grill:

My favorite restaurant
in Chicago
was gone this month.

Hard working Mexican guys
always generous portion
always clean
they opened
from 10:00 AM till 3:00 AM
everyday.

It's not their fault
Trump is bad
the economy is bad
probably
getting worse now.

Recession is on the way.

A shopping mall in Buffalo:

Buffalo, NY
is losing population
every year
a lot of shopping malls
had been closed out
by 2006.

During my college years,
I still remember
I visited one mall
almost 90% of its stores closed.

Still one pet food shop opened
full of products
two guys were standing
as if nothing happened.

They looked at me
I felt sorry for them.

Riccardo's:

A huge Pizzeria –
also an Italian restaurant
6,000 sf
up to $13,000 rent a month.

Waldo Garcia was the owner
a great man
almost 70 years old
married three times
five children
two grandkids.

Kathy is the last wife
a great lady
generous to give out a lot of foods
to neighbors and everyone.

Iconic place
closed out this year
after 30 years
shocking
even on the local news.

I cannot imagine
how they feel.

The space was divided
a new "Indian snack" and "Sports bar" came
just opened

apparently looking busy.

7 Luck:

A small Chinese take out
1,000 sf
The saddest place I have seen.

The owners have been changed
five times
since 2006.

The last owner
a small Chinese family
of three
decided to pour money in
expanded the space double

Not many guests really came
after one year renovation
horribly
COVID broke out

A new sushi restaurant
is there
now.

Gezim:

An Albanian oldman
75-years old
two sons
dishwasher
no English
but a very kind
generous guy.

He got eliminated
from the nursing home
because of COVID.

In this case
I am truly glad
the job was so hellish
with a small wage.

I am glad
he doesn't have to
suffer.

Life

of

Jim

(Poetry Book 5)

Life of Jim:

Jim (66) was our neighbor

The first time I met him was in 2013
when our family of 3 visited my condo
to purchase it with Mary
who was my real estate agent

A man

with broken glasses
holding broken laundry basket
came out to the aisle
to introduce himself
only until then
I felt good about him

There are only four units
on this floor
he had quarrels with
the Ukrainian couple
living in front of his unit
a lot, then

As time went on,
I truly wished he would go away

He threw out everything
to his door to make noise
whenever he got angry
by the couple

My cat and I got startled
whenever hearing the thunder

As time passed,
I was curious
if he was a hidden millionaire
just in case

No

he turned out to be nobody
paying off his small mortgage
($38,000)
over the course of 30 years

He finally died (66)
due to prostate cancer
a few years ago

He never had been married
left no child
no money
or even a photo of himself

I saw just a red bird
in his funeral photo

Yes
we can live like him
maybe that's what life is about

Or
we don't have to?

Extra:

My own near death experience

I got hit by a taxi
riding bicycle
when I was 10
which was 42 years ago

People said
I had been faint
unconscious
on the ground
for a couple of hours

Surprisingly,
nothing happened after that
no fracture or anything

I feel comfortable
whenever I think about it

In summary
I live an extra life now

I could have been dead
by then

Grandma:

She died when she was 94
a few years ago

She had been a burden
for the families
for long time

No income
had been generated by her
but she'd never stopped
moving her mouth

She tried to manipulate my life
trying to take advantage somehow
whenever having a chance

I assume
she did it to everyone

Everyone didn't like her
I didn't like her
I will never live like her

The Worst Human Being:

Sometimes, I see a person
who try to do
as many bad things as possible
before die

Jo Byeong-gap
in Joseon Dynasty
Kim jung-il in North Korea
Saddam Hussein in Iraq
Trump in America

Doing one more bad thing
before their deaths
seems to be their motto

Stupid to be busy
in old age,
to begin with

Mother-in-law:

Mother
who I never had a chance to meet
but who accepted me as her child

Rest in peace now

We all meet
in the end

Laureate

of

the Broke

(Poetry Book 6)

$5 Bus Scam:

Chicago pace buses
charges $2.25 for cash
although most commuters
use the Ventra card –
a convenient debit card
for public transportation

Occasionally,
I have seen people
asking drivers if they have changes
since all they have is a $5 bill
of course
there is no such a thing
like a change machine on the bus

I thought
they are in trouble
in the beginning
but realized that
there are too many people
asking the same question

Why do they always have a $5 bill?
Never $10 or $20?
No bank debit card,
although they can use it
as a Ventra card on the bus, too?

Once there was a boy shouting

since the driver rejected his free ride,
but getting extremely happy
when the driver changed his mind
seconds later

What kind of low lives
are they
trying to take a bus for free
and get extreme joy out of it?

I feel sorry for drivers
since they all know the trick
but always grant it

$15 Hair Cut:

I have gone to
Bella's hair salon
in Arlington Heights
for 15 years now

The first time I was there
it was $6 in 2015

Now finally $15
this year in 2025
although I always give them
$5 tip

The only difference is
another salon charging $40

opened in the same plaza
apparently
they look busy, too

Bella's still charges only $15:
Why?
I don't know
I feel sorry, but appreciating

Always full of hairdressers –
modest,
yet hard working Latinas

Lupe:

It was 2018
when I met Lupe –
a Latina
working in a nursing home

as a CNA

A struggling nursing student
living in South Chicago
renting a room
on the 3rd floor of a house
with her Puerto Rican boyfriend

Her parents got divorced
when she was a baby
her mom passed away
when she was a teen
her dad remarried,
having three sons separately

She got pregnant
when she was in early 20s
surprisingly, it was a black baby
her boyfriend left
real father of the baby
is completely unknown
forever

She met another Mexican,
who was young, but completely bald
another daughter was born
he always take a photo of
his own daughter only
on Facebook

Poor Lupe promiscuous

young Lupe two children
tired Lupe feeding babies
all live in California now

A Korean Old Man in Laos:

There is a Korean old man
in his 70s
bold
missing teeth
living countryside in Laos

Despite all,
he has a seemingly popular
YouTube channel

He's living with
a Laos girl in her 20s,
although she is a divorced mother
with one child

I don't know why
he had never married
until that age
while he'd lived in Korea
apparently, he doesn't seem to
have any family left there

The Laos village
looking extremely poor
no paved road
having traditional outhouses
outside home

Laos embassy officially warned
Koreans have done
too many sex travels
in the country
immigration to the country
is an extension of it

I wonder
when he is going to be
fed up with
his neverending poverty
for life

Thai Massage Girl Emily:

Emily is a single mother in her 40s
from Thailand
she worked at a massage spa
not very expensive
yet high quality
immaculately clean

Although she said she has two children
her Facebook always show
only her younger daughter
I don't know why

Her social media
was full of fantasy and fake
about her American life

I assume
someone in Thailand see these
although her mother
live in America with her

I don't know
where she works
any more.

Comfort

(Poetry Book 7)

Javier:

I opened my video game store
in 2006
in a nameless suburban strip mall
in Chicagoland

The Italian landlord,

who was also a lawyer,
was very sneaky

He suggested 3 month free rent
but took the amount of money
worth two month's rent
as a security deposit,
from where I got only 1 month's back
in the end
after the 8 years' contract was over

Javier was the first customer
Javier Martinez
a Mexican boy

After opening the store
I couldn't get a customer for 10 days
but he came with his mom
and bought 2 games
thankfully
then, he was an elementary student

He had been a great customer
for 8 years since then
his mom and brothers, too

By the time we closed out
our business 8 years later
he became a college boy
also delivering pizzas

He stopped by
at the last moment
and gave me a large deep dish pizza
with garlic topping

Later on,
his cousin Flores said
his entire family moved to
California
permanently

I cannot find Javier
any more,
as he is one of
those odd, but paradigmatic people
not having a Facebook account

Flores' account
is also deactivated
out of any reason now

Javier!

Wherever you live,
I wish my best luck!

Your family, too!

When we meet again,
pizzas are on me!

My Cat
who couldn't close his eyes:

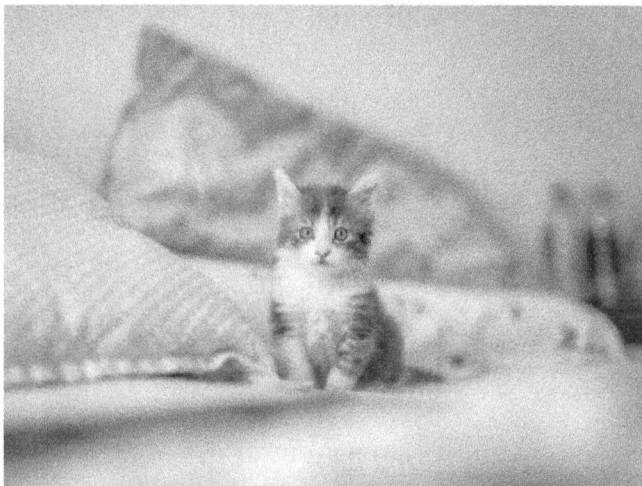

My cat was 2 month old
when he arrived at my apartment
in 2003

He died in 2020,
so I would say
he had lived a good life
in general

I remember one thing,
though

When I pet his head first time,
he couldn't close his eyes

He didn't move,
but he kept his eyes open

He didn't know
where he was
or who I am

After days passing by,
he left his eyes closed
comfortably
whenever I pet him

True comfort
finally arrived

Half Price Books:

This stupid store
pays the same amount for
cash and store credit
for used books

How come
could these be the same?

Store credit should be more
as in Gamestop –
I guarantee you that
HPB has no idea about
how the system works
overall

When I sold my books there
first time,
they tried to give $1 credit
for each books

Sometimes,
they gave me $2 or 3
for a book

I always took the store credit,
instead of cash,
to help them

I always bought a book
with the store credit
even when I don't need it
necessarily

Last time,
they gave me only $0.15
for 5 book –

rather old books
but in good condition

I don't know what happened –
it was a different guy
don't they have a fixed rule,
though?

Nonetheless,
I still tried to buy a poetry book
with that credit

However,
a different girl refused to give me
a discount,
which I hardly ask for

The poetry was
an extremely unpopular one
$5 on Amazon for a new –
$2 for an used one
I knew no one will buy it
except me

HPB insisted their price of $9
for an used one

I just took $0.15 cash
and left

No more!

Poor Love

(Poetry Book 8)

Poor Love:

Can your love survive?

A young girl,
whose parents passed away

due to car accident,
supporting her deaf grandma,
who has a debt from a loan shark

She worked in a company every day
and worked as a dishwasher every night

Incidentally,
she fell in love with her boss,
who had a family already

She is a drama heroine –
I had been in love with her
for about six months

Ariana:

Ariana was a young Latina (19)
she knew how to
take advantage of old men

She wasn't particularly pretty,
but she obviously knew
she was young, at least

She always addressed old men
to ask favors
and backed off immediately
when they needed her help

She had a fat butt

I guess
she kept it that way
intentionally,
as it seems to be popular
among young Latinas,
which I don't understand why

Carlos:

Carlos was
a short Mexican sous chef,
unnecessarily
rude and disrespectful
to dishwashers

Royal to the company,
beyond reason,
often in a humiliating way,
flattering upper management
all the time

However,
he didn't last very long –
not even a year
he lost his job much quicker

than I expected

I filed a complaint,
when the upper management
contacted me
for a survey
through my smartphone
I wonder if
that was why

Jazzercise:

Chris Smith (50)
was the most stupid
business woman
I've ever seen

Actually,
all three oldish
aerobics owners were

The internet cafe
next to my video game shop
was very slow
the owner guys were kind,
but actually
gave up on their business

The three women suddenly came,
out of nowhere,

and started discussing
their new business floor plan,
while the cafe was
still in business –
everyone found their act rude

In conclusion,
the cafe was gone,
but a new aerobics called
Jazzercise opened

However,
all they've made,
for the 5 years,
was extremely loud noise,
instead of money

They did it
without building
any proper noise insulation,
which brought me
a lot of pain

The landlord dropped
my rent to $1,100 a month (2014),
though I used to pay
up to $1,600 a month
before that business came

Regardless,
it must have damaged

their hearings a lot,
which was probably why
no one came

Author's Note

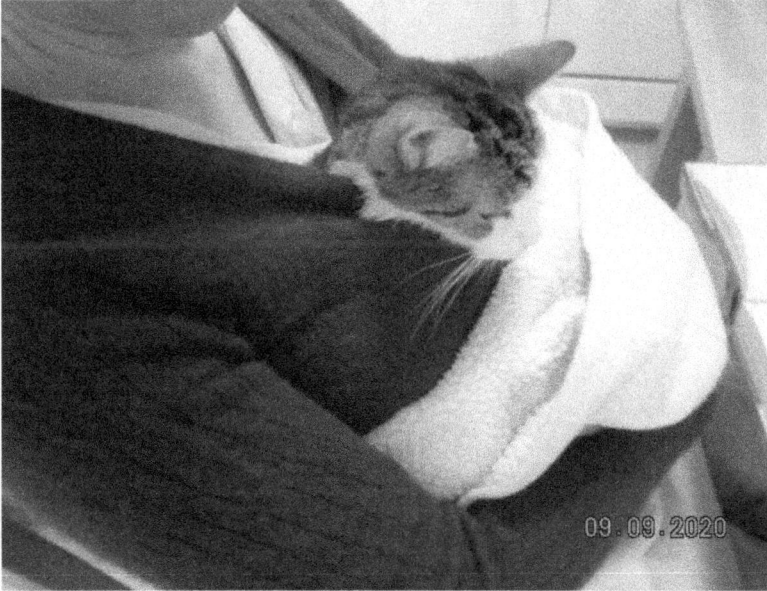

My wife holding Oscar (2020).

Congratulations: I truly appreciate you finishing my book until the end. *I would appreciate a* "one sentence review." I wish my best luck to you!

www.ingramcontent.com/pod-product-compliance
Lightning Source LLC
Chambersburg PA
CBHW021140020426
42331CB00005B/841